## Dedication

I dedicate this book to all of the Online Daters that are trying to find true love.

# Contents

# 5. Cars-Transportation

# 6. Job-Employment

# 7. X-Relationship's-Marriages

# 8. Family

# 9. Money

# 10. STD's

# Introduction

The Top 10 Things People Lie About on Online Dating Sites is a guide for men and women to help them in their pursuit of Love via Online Dating Sites.

Let's face it, there are thousands of Online Dating Sites today and most people meet their partners, husbands, wives, girlfriends, boyfriends, friends with benefits and lovers on Online Dating Sites. The reality is most people are too busy working or just too shy to approach someone on the street to actually go out and hunt down a mate. Thanks to the Internet, you can now find love online or anything else you are looking for.

I myself have been an Online Dater on and off since 2002. I have been on quite a few sites, some are not even around anymore because they have been bought out by the bigger names. This was way back when Online Dating was starting to get big. I think it is a great way to meet someone but you have to be very cautious.

I met my x-Husband on Match.com in 2002. He was the first guy I saw on there that I was attracted to. I didn't even bother looking around once I saw him. I contacted him first and needless to say he lied about almost everything and I was too naïve and ignored all of the warning signs. We dated for five years before we got married and he never really changed. He was a Cheater, Liar and a Manipulator who had a handful of women at his disposal at any given time that he used for different purposes. I was his 'Trophy Girlfriend/Wife' yet he had many other women around the entire time we were dating and married.

The whole disaster of the relationship was my fault because I allowed him to treat me that way and I kept forgiving him and taking him back. Yes, that's what I said, the whole thing was my fault because as soon as he lied the first time I should have got out and I didn't.

I have learned some hard lessons and the purpose of this book is to help my fellow Online Daters see and recognize the lies that people tell on their profiles and when dating online. I have learned that if someone lies about a little thing for example, where they live, they are hiding something and will lie about anything. It's up to you to weed out the dishonest Online Daters so you have a chance at finding true love.

Practically all the relationships I know are based on a foundation of lies and mutually accepted delusion.

Kim Cattrall

# 1

# Age

## I want to meet someone younger not older

Why do most people lie about their age? Because they think they
have to. Our culture at large -- embodies ageism. Young is good.
Older is less good is what most people think. One reason I think
people lie is because their preference is younger men or women.
My X-husband was seven years older and I found that he was a
bit boring, I still wanted to go out and do things and he had no
interest so in my mind a younger man (not too much younger)
would be perfect for me because I like to go out and do things so
dating a younger man is more realistic to me.

## I don't look or feel my age therefore I can lie about it

Another reason a person will lie about their age is they believe
they do not look their age. I know it sounds crazy and I think it is
a reality that some people just do not look their age therefore
they lie about it because they are in denial of their own mortality.
What is amusing is when they just go too far! I've seen people's
profiles where it is just embarrassing for them when I look at
their pictures and their age, they just don't match!  Remember a
lot of people's pictures are old and if they already look older in
their pictures then watch out because you will be in for a big
surprise when you finally do meet them.

This has happened to me several times where the man will say
he's one age and then when we meet they either look a lot older
and won't admit it or they come clean at the end of the date.

Seriously, I do not want to date a certain age range of men and when they lie they completely turn me off and waste my time. There are certain deal breakers and this is one of them for me.

## Money can't buy you love-Sugar Daddy/Mama Syndrome

Another reason people lie about their age is they purposely want someone a lot younger for their own ego. They want to look and feel younger so they believe a younger mate will take them back to their glory years. This actually can work out for some people and most of the time you see this scenario in Men that are going through a mid-life crisis. I know this sounds cliché but I happen to know this to be a clear fact and I know a few couples who are living this way. Personally, if I am not attracted to the person I don't care how much money they have or what they can 'offer' me, it just won't work for me. I have had a few offers to live this sort of lifestyle and I even tested it out a couple of times with no luck. I just couldn't do it. I would rather be alone than be with an older man to take care of me that I am not attracted to in the least. Life is too short to be unhappy and we all know money can't buy you love.

## Mid Life Crisis

**Definition of a Mid-life crisis:** a term coined in 1965 by Elliott Jaques stating a time where adults come to realize their own mortality and how much time is left in their life. A midlife crisis is experienced by many people during the midlife transition when they realize that life may be more than halfway over. Sometimes, a crisis can be triggered by transitions experienced in these years, such as andropause or menopause, the death of parents or other causes of grief, unemployment or underemployment, realizing that a job or career is hated but not knowing how else to earn an equivalent living, or children leaving home. People may reassess their achievements in terms of their dreams. The result may be a desire to make significant changes in core aspects of day-to-day life or situation, such as in career, work-life balance, marriage, romantic relationships, large expenditures, or physical appearance.

Mid-life crisis has been a real issue in the world for many years and chances are this will never change. This is where you see the 50+ men and women in their sport cars, toupees, extensions and plastic surgery waltzing around town or in bars looking for a younger partner.

The reason I see this is an issue is because we are all different ages and for a good reason, I mean what does a 55 year old man have in common with a 25 year old young lady? Please give me one good reason besides sex because frankly when men get in their mid-50's and up they often need a little help with their sexual activities and if they say different I beg to differ. And let's not even talk about binging babies into the equation because that is just plain stupid in my opinion. Not to mention the existing kids that are probably the same age or older than the girlfriend/boyfriend arm candy. I just don't see this as a healthy relationship. I cannot even imagine dating a man that is even 10 years older than myself!

Age and life experience is important in making a good match. You must have things in common besides sex and we all know it takes more than love and sex to make a relationship work.

A person should closely monitor the pictures people post and always ask them their age before you go out even if it is on their profile, putting them on the spot will give them the opportunity to come clean before you go out. If they don't come clean and you meet them in person and they don't look their age, then that is a big RED FLAG that something is just not right with this person and you should walk away. Often, one lie leads to another and another and so on. Don't let this one go and ignore it, trust me you will be sorry in the end if you do.

Another thing that I see a lot on Men's profiles that are over 50 is that they would like to have children. I think it is a little too late to be having kids when you are that old. Kids need their parents to be around and this is just not a good idea. Most kids, and I hate to say it but here goes, will be embarrassed to have a Dad that looks like their grandpa.

# Cougars

A woman will lie about her age if she is a 'cougar', meaning she is attracted to younger men. I myself must admit that I too like younger men (not too much younger) and have been called a cougar by my own daughter. She also referred to me as Mrs. Robinson... LOL

The word 'cougar' is a term used to refer to a growing number of middle-aged women who are Online Dating Sites, frequent clubs and bars in order to meet and have a sexual relationship with younger men.

Some people say that being a cougar reveals a sense of desperation, others say being a cougar is a source of self-empowerment, in which older women reclaim the dating scene and prove once again that they're still attractive and alluring. Some young men are attracted to a cougar because they see the relationship as being a 'no strings attached,' giving them the green light to explore certain aspects of intimacy and sex that a woman their own age would never be able to give without having to have a long term commitment.

I get a lot of propositions from younger men all the time that are looking for a cougar on Dating Sites. The men say they can provide me with all I need and want in a sexual relationship and that they only date older women because women their own age are just too immature and expect too much. This is what they tell me at least.

Most of my X-husband's 'other women' were older than him. I can understand this now as I am getting older however; there is a difference in being 'desperate and needy' and just enjoying the company of a younger man. My X-husband's 'other women' were older and very unattractive and would have given their last dime just to spend some time with him, it was actually a very sick and unhealthy relationship they had with him. I am clearly not like that at all.

Let's move on...

# 2

# Weight-Height

## I only gained a 'few' pounds!

This is a very sensitive topic but so very important to point out and discuss. I have heard this from both men and women, mostly men though. I hear this all too often 'I showed up and didn't even recognize her', 'she looked nothing like her pictures', 'I was so embarrassed I almost walked away', I was so embarrassed I walked away', and 'I was shocked and I told her this isn't going to work'. Ladies, this is the main complaint I get from guys.

I'm not singling out the women on here because the same thing happened to me on an Online Date (POF). The guy showed up and was probably 75 pounds over the weight he was in his pictures. It was quite a scene he even drove a little white Mercedes and I am not even sure how he fit in that car. I don't mean to be disrespectful but it was quite comical to me at the time. I mean sometimes you just have to have a sense of humor and expect the unexpected.

Back to the ladies. Guys, ladies lie about their weight simply because we don't think you would date us if you thought we were overweight. That's it! It's real simple. Guys, stop obsessing about the reason why they do it because the truth is everyone lies about their weight whether it be on their driver's license or whatever. Unless, you are the perfect size and weight proportionate chances are this is going to happen.

Since hearing this all the time from men I kinda get where when you are talking online via the dating site they request a full length body shot. This to me is a very annoying request but I get why they are asking now. I bet there are 0% of women that request a full shot from a man (just sayin).

Another annoying request is when you finally give them your digits and then they request this 'Take a picture right now the way you are and send it to me' HUH? Really? Half the time I am not picture worthy I mean this is not the Real Housewives of Orange County where we are always made up with hair and make-up even in the morning. This just doesn't happen but on TV. Can't we just get a guy to love us just the way we are?

A male friend told me that guys are 'visual' and so they got it in their heads we are always going to look like a magazine model. They are on Fantasy Island most of the time because we are just women. We like to eat, we gain weight now and then and most of us are not a size '2'.

I can understand being lied to about someone's weight and I am not excusing that at all. I absolutely think that we should put our real weight on the Online Dating Profile with a recent photo just to eliminate the unnecessary going nowhere dates. Life is too short to waste anyone's time and to be honest just think how much better it would be for us if a guy or girl knew exactly what they were getting before we go out and liked us anyway? What a concept. I personally wouldn't want to be with a guy if he expected me to be a size '2' and look like a cast member from the Real Housewives of Orange County all the time.

# Real Men Like Curves

In today's world it is so typical to believe that you have to be a size '2' for the ladies and for the guys, you have to have that 'six pack' in order to be in a happy relationship. This is in part due to the reality shows, magazines and movies. In a perfect world this would be true but for the normal person this is just not realistic. I believe most people really try to fit the stereotype of society but it is truly not an easy thing to do. Don't get me wrong, I believe that everyone should exercise and eat right to be healthy but everyone is just different.

Everyone has different genes and therefore not everyone can be the perfect size as seen on TV. This is why plastic surgeons have made it so big in this world today. Everyone wants to look better and some will even pay to make themselves look better. I have nothing against having plastic surgery. I myself have had some work done and I believe it does help me feel better about myself but I am single and ready to mingle so looking good is a goal of mine. If I would have stayed married to my first husband, then I am 100% positive I would not have had any plastic surgery.

Let's talk about 'Curves'. I totally believe that most men love curvy women. I don't know of any men that would want a woman that has a little boys figure. I think curves are sexy and I think most men do too. Problem is society will only show ladies on TV, reality shows and magazines who are a size '2' with curves. (Curves added by plastic surgery)

In my entire life I have averaged from a size 2 to a size 8. It varies on and off but I have been a size 6 and under for most of my life but there have been times I have gotten heavier. I hate to say it but most of the time I was above a size 6 was when I was married or in a relationship. Those days are gone now because I work out and eat healthy so I am happy at the weight I am.

Men and women who have partners who are a little or a lot heavier than they would like, my advice would be to encourage them and not to belittle them. Encouragement always works better and is so much nicer. If you belittle the person because they are overweight then it will only backfire on you and it just isn't nice.

When you love who you are as a person, you will be so much

more lovable and attractive to everyone else. The happier you are and self-confident the more people will be drawn to you and that doesn't mean you have to be a size '2' to attain it. Just exercise if you are able and eat healthy and you will feel better whatever size you are. After all 'You are what you eat' and if you eat nothing but junk food then you will feel like junk! Be good to yourself, you deserve it!

## Height-Just tell the truth

People lie about their height simply because they want to be taller or shorter than they actually are. It's a pretty simple reason why someone would lie about their height.

Personally, I think this is one of the worst things about Online Dating Sites. I have experienced that 99% of the men I have dated have lied about their height. It is very annoying to me because I like to wear heels and I am already 5'6. With my heels on, that makes me 5'9 or taller. I like taller men, that is just my preference and when a Man lies to me about his height it really turns me off automatically when I see them in person. Honestly, there are a lot of nice looking HOT men out there that are a bit shorter than my taste and I still won't date them.

The same goes for the women. They lie about their height too. The reason might be because they would like to be taller and think that the guys will like them more if they are taller, or simply because they are super tall already and won't think a guy will like them because they may be taller than him. Look at Nicole Kidman for example. She was married to Tom Cruise and now Keith Urban and they are both shorter than her but it doesn't seem to bother her at all. I say, good for her I wish I could do that but I can't. No offense to the shorter people at all.

The funny thing is when someone does lie about their height, do they really think we are not going to notice when we finally meet in person? This happens to me all the time. The worst was a man named John. He said on his profile he was 5'11. I met him in person with my heels on and when I went to hug him to say hello, I had to bend down which means he was only about 5'8. That's a huge difference! Immediately I knew it was not going to go well and he also lied about other things too that I quickly figured out during the night. Seriously, I would not have even answered his initial message back to me if I would have known. Consequentially I have learned that I just simply cannot trust a man when he gives his height on his Online Dating Profile unless he is over 6'1. If they say they are 6'1 and over, then they usually are not lying about their height. From my past experiences about men lying about their height, I will only date men that state they are 6'1 and over. Mind you, I'm not wasting my time anymore without knowing for sure they are as tall as I would like. Sorry guys…

## My Advice

My advice would be before you go out with the person, ask them over the phone how tall they are even if it is already on their profile. This will give them an opportunity to come clean before the date if they are lying and if they don't come clean before the date and are not the height they say they are, end the date early and never go out with them again. Even though it is possible that the only thing they are lying about is their height but why take the chance? There are millions of people on dating sites and you just have to invest the time if you are going to meet the right person. This means going out on dates and wasting time but in the end it could be worth it. You may even make a new friend who knows?

Just put down your real weight and post a recent picture so the guy or girl can love you for who you are, after all you are worth it and deserve to be with a guy or girl that is realistic. You should always expect the person to be a little heavier in person than their pictures. It's just realistic and then you won't be disappointed. If you cannot picture him or her with a few pounds on before you go out, then don't waste anyone's time and move on.

I must say that it is never OK to be rude to someone, always be polite but stand by what you are really looking for. Any date should never end badly or even ugly just because the person lied about their height UNLESS they are rude, obnoxious, drunk or under the influence then you can be whatever you want, just get the hell out of there!

# 3

# Single Status

## They are Not Single

Let's talk about why people lie about their 'Single Status' on Online Dating sites. I have come across this many times when Online Dating in fact my x-husband had many women he was dating at the time when I met him. This is the scary part of Online Dating. People can lie and fabricate anything on their profiles these days and I don't see that changing anytime soon. This is why you will need to be very cautious when you are Online Dating.

The reason people lie about their 'Single Status' is because they are looking for someone else to add to their bundle of men or women. They have 'The Grass Is Greener on the Other Side' attitude and mentality. Or, they are simply just 'Players' looking for as much action as they can possibly get.

I know several women that this has happened to. All of the guys had girlfriends already and were just looking for some action on the side. Unfortunately, a lot of women and men get fooled because they simply do not check up on the person when they begin dating them. A lot of them will make you believe that you are 'Exclusive' so they can get what they can from you but they are in no way 'Exclusive' with you in their own minds.

When I met my x-husband, he asked me to be 'Exclusive' on date 3. I totally believed and assumed he would take his profile down from Match.com but he didn't. Luckily for me I had my BFF checking the sites for him. We found him on several different dating sites while we were supposed to be 'Exclusive'. He was not very smart, he used the same Username on every site so it was easy to find him. I did confront him about it and he flat out lied and I believe he said he 'forgot' he was on there, that his 'brother' was using his profile to meet women or that it must be a glitch in their system because he did take himself off but they must have made a mistake and left it up. Believe me, I heard every excuse he could possibly think of and I was so stupid and in love that I let it go. Then he would say he deleted his profile and he would just create a brand new one with a new Username! This was exhausting and went off and on for years. Stupid me, I should have dumped him the first time he lied. That was a huge mistake and the reason I am writing this book. I hope people will read this and learn that when someone lies about their 'Single Status' that is a huge red flag that should not be ignored.

I have even received messages from men that flat out admit they are not 'single' but they are looking for an 'open relationship' or some 'fun'. Really? I had this one guy I met on POF that would just not give up after I told him several times I am not into 'open relationships'. He still to this day messages me. I could block him but I am learning a lot from him and his mind set that I just let him go on and on why I should give in to him. Give me a BREAK! It's so cliché, the more I turn him down, the more he comes back. This is so typical. If I would have agreed to go out with him on his very first attempt, who knows he could have got bored and discarded me like I am sure he is doing to most women. It a psychological thing with them. They say they don't want a relationship but in fact they are looking for the girl that is so hard to get so they can BE in a relationship. I know it doesn't make sense but it is true.

I have met several men and women that have said they wish there was a website they could look someone up before they go out with them. Well, I took this to heart and decided to create one. Lindasdatelist.com is a site where you can look someone up and also write a review about a dangerous person, a player, a drunk or drug abuser, domestic violence abuser or anything else that you would think someone else should know about the person. This is all free. I think it is way too important for someone to know what other people think about the person they met online. It's like the 'Angies List' of Online Dating.

An example would be if you see someone on the Dating Site while you are browsing that you know is in a relationship, married, a domestic violence abuser, drunk or drug addict, or anything else that is dangerous, you should definitely report them to the Online Dating site and Lindasdatelist.com. This gives Online Daters some insight of the person they might date before they go out. You can totally be anonymous too. In the same realm, if you meet a really great person but the attraction is just not there, you can write a nice review about the person. I believe a website like Lindasdatelist.com is way overdue and should be utilized if you are Online Dating.

## A Plenty Of Fish Dating Story

I want to tell you about a guy I met on POF. He was a good looking, tall and charming guy. We met and started dating. He told me he took his profile down and yes I checked and it was gone. We had an on and off again relationship for about a year simply because he was 'not available' all the time. I knew something wasn't right but I invested myself emotionally and I did end up getting hurt even though I did not want a serious relationship, I still ended up getting hurt and the relationship ended badly.

Some of the warning signs of why I would not pursue a boyfriend/girlfriend relationship with him is because he would do things like turn his phone off while we were together. He wouldn't take any calls. Now I am not stupid I saw right through this in the beginning. Obviously he was hiding something. I never really took him seriously but eventually after spending time together I started getting some feelings for him. We would have some arguments and immediately he would put his profile back up on the Dating Site.

After I created my website, I started getting reviews about HIM! Several women he had told about my site Lindasdatelist.com had reported him on there as being a 'player' and other things. This is what happens when you lie about things, they eventually come back to bite you in the Ass. LOL. He totally gave himself away and had several women on the side he was seeing at the same time.

Seriously, I could have been hurt real bad but because I saw the warning signs in the beginning and never took the relationship serious, I got hurt for a short time but not damaged. I find the entire story amusing and hilarious. Now the good part is, he is on the site and anyone can look him up and read about him before going out with him. He never had me fooled and honestly I only wanted to see him on my terms and timeframe anyway so it worked out for me at the time. I was in control the entire time because I knew he was lying from the very beginning and therefore, I was not surprised when I finally found out. Yes, I could have just broke things off with him in the beginning but I was having fun with him and so I let it go on. Maybe I was wrong but I don't regret anything about that relationship, he is just a guy that needs to 'grow up' and just settle down with one person. Not my problem, I had clear eyes the entire time so I was not fooled.

## My Advice

My advice about people who lie about their relationship status would be this: When you meet someone online and are in an 'Exclusive Relationship', look around other dating sites and see if the person is still online. Note that I said IF you are in an 'Exclusive' relationship meaning both parties have agreed to be 'Exclusive'. If you are just dating the person and getting to know them then it is OK for them to still be on the Dating Site.

I know this sounds a little crazy to some people who think they should just 'trust' the person when they tell you they took themselves off of the Dating Site, but I'm sorry this Online

Dating is a crapshoot and you never know what you are going to get. Don't trust anyone until they earn it! If you find the person is lying about their single status, report them to the Dating Site and report them to Lindasdatelist.com so that other people will know what they are getting themselves into and definitely do not continue to date them, this will avoid any chance of getting hurt later after you invested your time, energy and emotions into someone who is not truthful.

# 4

# Addictions

## A Hidden Secret—Smoking

Most people today have some sort of addiction whether it be shopping, drugs, alcohol, pills, cars, shoes, TV/Cable shows or even another person.

Some of these addictions listed above are not dangerous but can be a problem in any relationship even for single people. Let's talk about the drug and alcohol addictions including smoking. I went out on a POF date with a guy who clearly stated in his profile that he was a non-smoker. Being a smoker is a definite deal breaker for me even now that marijuana is legal for some people I still will not date a guy who smokes anything but a cigar (once in a while).

When the guy showed up at the bar I went in to hug him hello and I totally could smell the nicotine on his breath. The guy wasn't even smart enough to put a mint in his mouth before he got in the bar! After we sat down and ordered a drink, he said he needed to go out and smoke a cigarette. I asked him then 'didn't you say you were a non-smoker in your profile'? He answered back and said 'Yes I did, but that's the only thing I lied about'. The only thing?? Really?? To most people that are non-smokers that is a clear deal breaker. Again, a waste of my time and energy to get all prettied up to meet him... Turns out the evening took an even worse turn. This is why when people lie about things, it is usually the beginning of even more bad things to come and I found out later this was true.

We had a couple drinks, I thought well I have nothing else to do so maybe I'll just stay a little while. I excused myself to the bathroom. When I came back, he quickly said to me, 'Let's go down the street to the other bar' and he actually hurried me out of there! I was not sure what was going on until we got about 20 yards outside from the front door and the bartender comes running out saying 'Sir, sir, you forgot to pay your bill'! I could have just died! I was so embarrassed and not to mention the street was very busy with people whom I am sure got a good laugh out of us. At that point he opened his wallet and all I saw was a $20.00 bill. I didn't see any credit cards or anything else. He reluctantly gave her the $20.00 and turned and walked away. I am not even sure how much the bill was but I do know that's all the money he had. RED FLAG!

At this point you would think I would have just walked away but this was getting interesting so we walked to the bar down the street and guess what? His bartender friend was working and we got a free drink… LOL… Needless to say I never went out with him again but that was quite an experience.

This could have all been avoided if he didn't lie on his profile. If his profile stated 'smoker' than clearly I wouldn't have went out with him. But, people lie and this is what happens sometimes but you can see how one lie led to so many other things on the first date! Obviously the guy was down on his luck and this is just not the time to date someone if you are down on your luck.

## Alcohol

A lot of people are alcoholics. This is an addiction and unless you are an alcoholic actively participating in AA, it is not something that everyone is going to admit. This is something you will have to be aware of as you are dating someone. I believe meeting for the first time it is OK to meet for a drink. It lightens the mood and makes things a little smoother. This is the time you need to get your radar on to see if the person has a problem with alcohol. It is pretty easy to spot. If they get drunk on the first date then that is a pretty decent sign that this person might have a drinking problem. I wouldn't discount it though (unless they act disorderly or inappropriate) but if they don't, they may just be nervous. This is entirely possible and you really should give the person a second chance. If on the second date the same thing happens, well then there is your answer. By the way, a person active in AA program is advised to not be in a relationship until they are sober for one year.

## Other Women/Men or Both

Another addiction could be a woman or a man. A womanizer is a Man that has to have a lot of women giving his attention to him at the same time. Same goes for a Manizer (my term for the opposite of a womanizer). Being a Womanizer/Manizer is an addiction. I believe with my whole heart that this is an addiction. The old saying goes 'once a cheater, always a cheater'. They never really grow out of it and I speak from experience.

My x-husband was a womanizer. He needed as many women 'in the wings' at all times even when we were married. This was an ego boost for him. He was a very handsome man but he was insecure. He needed to hear how great he was from all kinds of women or he just didn't feel complete. He would flirt with women at work (I saw the emails) and he didn't care if they were married or anything. He kept all his x-girlfriends at bay who would call him on holidays and birthdays and bring him gifts and everything. Lord only knows why I put up with this! He was a liar. He lied about his 'Single Status' in the very beginning and I should have known then to walk away but I didn't. He turned out to be a very bad guy who tried to do a lot of bad things to me after we separated. This is why I tell you one lie turns into more bad things as you get to know the person.

I hear this from my male gay friends. They tell me they get hit on by married men all the time. This is very scary for me because I want my man to be faithful. This does happen and for the most part they certainly aren't going to admit it, so this is something a man will lie about and I am sure the same is true about women.

# Illegal Drugs and Prescription Pills

This seems like a no brainer but if the guy or girl uses illegal drugs period or prescription pills (excessively) then they clearly have an addiction. Drug addicts are liars, thieves, manipulators and abusers. Drugs go hand in hand with domestic violence as well. Most all of the people in prison all have something to do with drugs. They were either selling drugs, using drugs or both and it ended with them in jail or prison. Nothing good can come out of a drug user. If you see this happening with a person you are dating, get out immediately!

## My Story

I met a guy whom I married. I did not meet him online but I met him in a bar. He smoked pot and I let it go. I got pregnant (unplanned) and we ended up getting married. After being married a year or so I found out he was using Crystal Meth all the time. He would get high and we would fight, he beat me up a couple times before I got out of it and left him. To this day he is living on the streets and has been in and out of jail for years and he never stopped the drugs. Unfortunately, my son started going down the same path as his father and this is clearly my fault. I should have walked away from his Dad the minute I found out he was using marijuana and this would have never happened. I love my son and would not give him up for the world but I regret who his Dad is and I picked him! It's a very sad story.

## My Advice

My advice on addiction is stay away from Online Daters who have an addiction at all costs. Do not tolerate it under any circumstance and never bring kids around or get pregnant from/with a person who has an addiction. The kids are the ones who suffer the worst and it is just not fair to them.

# 5

# Cars-Transportation

## Do You Have a Car?

I love the Online Dating Sites that have the 'Do you have a car?' as a question for the Online Dater. What I don't love is that this is a huge thing that people lie about. The reason someone would like about this is they just don't have their life in order at the moment and they do not want to admit that. There are exceptions to this and they are, maybe you live in New York City where no one really needs a car there. I can see that geographically there would be an exception to this. Anywhere a person doesn't need a car then this is not a big deal however; for example, if you live in Southern California then you really do need a car in order to get by.

So, as an Online Dater when I read someone's profile I always look at the 'Do you have a car' answer to make an assessment if this is someone I even want to talk to. I have seen answers like 'Prefer not to say'? HUH? Obviously that is like pleading 'No Contest' in court... LOL

What really makes me mad is when they say they have a car yet when you go to meet them, they want you to pick them up? This happened to me before and stupidly I did go and pick the person up. I should have known when he asked me to pick him up that he really didn't have his life in order and I was right, he didn't. This is something now that I just will not ignore. That guy was very good looking and fun to be around but he just didn't have his life in order at that time.

At my age, I do not want to have to be someone's sugar mama or taxi service so if they don't have a car then to me that is a huge red flag. I do not want to date anyone who doesn't have their life in order. Not that I am perfect (far from it) but I do have my life in order and I want to meet someone who is on the same page as myself.

I talked to another guy on a Dating Site, we never met in person and this is why. I asked him what kind of car he drove (this is standard for me now because I have been lied to before) and he proceeded to tell me how his 1983 Mercedes blew up on the freeway and his friend gave him a car. OK, without sounding too critical here to me that was a red flag. I mean I am not rich but if my car blew up and I couldn't afford to lease a new one or even buy a used car by myself then I have problems. I believe this guy just didn't have his life in order at the time so I ended it at the end of that call. I was not even going to go any further because I simply do not trust anyone until they have earned it. I believe this saved me from making any mistakes later because I just accessed his situation and compared it to mine and made a decision not to go there.

There are millions of people on dating sites so eliminating one for not having a car is not a big deal because there are more fish in the sea to choose from.

## My Advice

My advice would be if you meet someone who clearly states on their profile that they have a car but they really don't, do not go out with them. If they are lying about having a car, they will lie about anything else. If they admit up front they do not have a car, it's up to you whether you want to go out and be the taxi service but I am highly against it because like I said, if they do not have a car then they most likely do not have their life in order and you should really only date someone who is at the same stage in life as you are. Note: there could be a reason why the person doesn't have a car and it could be because they were caught driving drunk or under the influence which would open the door for many other problems like addiction. This is very likely… just sayin...

# 6

# Job-Employment

## Occupation

People lie about their Occupations/Employment because if they do not have a job, they don't want to appear to be a loser. Let's face it, these days just about everyone needs a job to make ends meet. If you have no job, then society will view you as either 'rich' or a 'loser', or 'lazy'.

Some people just cannot work due to disabilities and I can understand that. That's why we have the government and tax payers to help support the disabled and even the underprivileged but this is not what this book is about so we will save that topic for another time.

Most dating sites have a field on the profiles for 'occupation'. Most people fill this out but there are the others that skirt around the subject and will write things like 'fortune teller', 'circus leader' and I have even seen 'I make $ so who cares'? That is an interesting one because I actually met the person who put 'I make $ so who cares'? He actually didn't have a job at all and struggled day to day to get by.

I totally understand how life has it's up's and down's and sometimes people get laid off, fired, sick or something else that forces them out of their job and they are actively looking for a new one. That's just life, I get that but to flat out lie and say you have a job when you don't is again like I said just a little white lie that will lead to many more I guarantee it.

Some of the occupations that people put on their profiles I try to stay away from because they are not stable jobs and when someone struggles with money it is just not a good start to any relationship. I want to know the person can fully support themselves without any help from anyone else. I do not sign up for these dating sites to find someone to support. One of the Occupations that I stay clear of is 'contractor'. I find that 99% of the 'contractors' that I have met online are struggling day to day from job to job. This is usually a big red flag for someone like me that this person really just doesn't have their lives in order. Of course there are exceptions to this and it could be that the person owns the company and is very successful.

It is a fact that most marriages and relationships end due to money problems therefore, it is a good idea to pay close attention this on the person's profile.

## My Advice

My advice would be this: If you are a serious Online Dater who is truly looking for love and even marriage, then the person having a job and a way to support themselves (legally) is a big deal. The exception to this may be a Man or Woman who is financially stable enough and doesn't care about the person they meet having a job then good for them. I myself am not looking for a 'Sugar Daddy' or someone to support me, I want to find a life partner and to me my life partner is someone who has their life in order.

I am just doing the math here and trying to help people see and understand the lies that people tell on their Online Dating Profiles and to understand that it is a crap shoot out there in the Online Dating world and you will need to be real careful and weed out the people that are just not right for you.

# 7

# X-Relationships-Marriages

## You Have Been Married How Many Times?

The 'Longest Relationship' question is an important one on the Online Dating Profile page. This is something everyone needs to pay attention to and the reason I say this is because if the person is over 40 and hasn't been in a long term relationship over 5 years then there may be a commitment issue. By the time I hit 40, I had been married and divorced a few times. I got married the first time at 18. I can totally understand how this could happen to many people these days because people change so much as they get older. I only know a few couples that have been married to the same person for over 20 years.

Someone that does not have long term relationships is someone that has commitment issues and this is a red flag to someone like me. Some people are not serious about finding love and they just want to date and have fun, this scenario may work for them however; I do know that as a woman, when I get intimate with a Man I want a commitment. Women have a hard time separating their feelings and sex. For Men this is different, it takes them longer to get emotionally involved yet they are ready and willing to have sex right away. I highly advise against getting sexually intimate before being in a committed relationship with someone. Of course you are going to run into the people who want to test drive the car before buying it and this is a dangerous place to be because one or both parties can get hurt.

Let's talk about when you get the question 'Are you friendly with your X'? This is a question that I often get asked by a guy. I am not sure why they would ask this except maybe they want to know if you still talk to your X thinking that maybe you are still sexually involved with him/her. I think this is a question that shouldn't be asked on the first few dates and I will tell you why. When you give someone too much personal information on the first couple of dates or even over the phone before you go out, you are taking a big risk because the chances of a real relationship with the person are pretty low. It takes a lot of dating before you meet that person you really have a connection with. Don't be giving out all your dirty laundry about your life to anyone especially a total stranger you meet on an Online Dating site. It's none of their business really. And just because someone asks you a personal question, don't ever feel obligated to answering it if you are not comfortable. People will want to know your entire life history before they will invest and get involved.

If you tell a total stranger that for example your X stole all your money, cheated on you and tried to hire someone to kill you when you first meet them, chances are they will run for the hills. How could you blame them if they did? They don't need to know your X is psycho and still emails you and is late on his spousal support and you are seeing a therapist and on Xanax to relieve the anxiety you have! This is just too much information to give out to a total stranger.

Everyone has baggage and drama in their lives and I love the people who put on their bios 'Must be Drama Free'... This is just so laughable because life experiences are what make us who we are today and most people learn and get better from them. I truly wouldn't want to meet someone who has had a 'Drama Free' life! They would never understand a crisis when it comes up in real life. Everyone goes through storms in their life and you need someone with you that can understand and be supportive.

## Crazy And Dangerous X's

If you have a crazy or dangerous X that can be harmful to a new boyfriend or girlfriend in your life, you will need to ensure that the proper steps are taken so that you do not endanger anyone. Even if that means that you do not date until it is safe than that is what you need to do. Do not ever endanger anyone else because of a crazy or dangerous X.

# 8

# Family

## Embarrassed of Family Members

No family is perfect. There is always one or more 'Black Sheep' in every family. When you meet someone online this is one of the topics of conversation 'your family'. First it's do you have any children? How old are your children? Do they live with you? Do they go to school or work? Are you on speaking terms with your X? Do they have the same father? I get asked all these questions every time I get into a conversation on the first date or even on our first phone conversation. Talking about your past is always a difficult thing to do especially if there is some dirty laundry or secrets. I always say this to people, do not give out your entire family history on the first few dates. These people you meet online are total strangers and you may never even see them again!

Meeting people online is like filling out a verbal resume. People want to know all the bad things and baggage you may have so they can take off running at the first sign of you not being perfect. Frankly, I find it very rude for someone to 'interview' you on the first few dates. I like to keep my personal business aside especially when it comes to my children. Many people these days have been married more than once and may have children from both marriages or even never married with kids. This is happening more and more these days. People live longer and therefore the chances of being married more than once is very high. I happen to have 2 kids from 2 marriages. What is the big deal? I hate answering the question 'Are they from the same father'? Well, maybe I just don't want to divulge that information to a total stranger and besides it's none of their business unless we become a couple. Am I embarrassed? Not embarrassed about my children but maybe a little embarrassed that I made some mistakes although it has made me who I am today and I am proud of that.

## Family Members with Mental Illness, Addictions or Criminal Records

Another question is 'Are you close with your family'? This is a tough one because many people including myself have some family members that we are not speaking to for various reasons. Does that make me a bad person? NO! I am sure everyone has a valid reason for not speaking to one or more family members and again this is none of their business unless we become a couple and are dating exclusive. They do not need to know that your sister is 'mentally unstable' or your brother has 'money problems' or even your own children may have addiction problems and have maybe been in and out of jail. These examples are very plausible these days and happen a lot more than people think. This doesn't mean that you are a bad person it just means that you are normal.

We have children that might get into trouble. This is a fact of the general population these days. Just because your children have made bad choices does not make you a bad parent. These days almost everyone has to work and cannot be around their children 24/7 to supervise them. There are many single parents trying to raise their children on their own and this goes without saying that it is the toughest thing to do being a single parent, working and trying to provide for your children. This is not information that you would want to disclose on the first few dates with a total stranger you meet online. Save this for later if the person seems worthy enough to know your personal business. If after hearing all of your 'dirty laundry' they decide it is too much for them then fine let them go because they are not the right person for you. This in no way means that you are lying or holding back information, it just means that these Online Daters are total strangers and you will need to protect yourself and your family.

If and when you meet someone that you become exclusive with, then I believe it is your obligation to inform them of anything that could be harmful to them. For example, if you have a child that is a drug addict and comes over to your house often then this is something that your boyfriend/girlfriend will need to know about for their own protection.

# Religion

When you are viewing someone's profile on a dating site, please notice the field where it states your 'religion'. Many times people will put 'other' on their profiles. This to me is suspicious but who knows these days there are many different religions out there but my question to you is, wouldn't you want to know this piece of information before you decided to go out with someone?

This happened to me once. I actually did go out with a man who had 'other' in the religion box. After a few dates he discloses to me that he converted to Judaism. This is all fine and dandy for him but clearly on my profile it states my religion and the two do not mix well. If I had known or thought to ask what his religion was, I would not have wasted my time and energy on dating him.

For some people they just don't care but for me this is a big deal in fact it is a deal breaker. People who lie about their religion or do not disclose it on their Online Dating profile are hiding something and my advice would be to always ask if they do not disclose it on their profile if it is important to you before you go out.

My opinion is that you should only date people of your own religion because you will have the same beliefs and core values as someone from your same religion. If you get married and have kids and you are not of the same religion, how are you going to raise your kids? I think the children get confused and who is going to win the argument of what religion to raise your kids in? This can become a breakdown in the marriage and cause many problems so it is best to avoid it from the beginning.

# 9

# Money

## Income Question On Their Profile

People will lie about how much or how little money they have for various reasons. On a person's Online Dating profile there is a field for 'income'. A person can choose how much they make or simply click 'prefer not to say'. I personally do not put my income in that field because I do not want anyone to know my income. It's as simple as that. I always have to remind myself that what you put on your profile in the internet world is public information. A person must be super cautious when putting any personal information on their profiles. On the other hand, when I see a man's profile and they put 'prefer not to say' I look directly at their 'occupation'. Depending on the 'occupation' I will then decide whether I want to communicate with this person or not. If they have no answer on the 'occupation' then to me this is a red flag. It usually means they have no job.

## Eliminate Gold Diggers

Some people do not put their income on their Online Dating Profiles because they do not want to attract the infamous 'gold digger'. I can totally understand this. Sadly to say there are many Online Daters scamming the Dating sites looking for a Sugar Mama or Sugar Daddy. This is something that you will have to figure out for yourself. An example would be let's say you meet a guy online and decide you want to meet him in person. Depending on where you want to meet, pay attention to how he treats you. Is he generous? Does he offer to buy an appetizer along with a cocktail or if you meet for coffee, does he offer to buy you a pastry? Does he pay for your valet parking? If they don't even offer that, I would be concerned. Either they do not have the funds for the extras or they do not want to invest in the relationship. Maybe they are just not that into you. This is easy to tell especially if they only want to stay for one drink and then they have to go. That's not a problem if there is no chemistry you simply say goodbye and maybe gain a friend in the process however; if you make it to a second date and he does not take you to eat at a decent restaurant or take you on a fun outing, then I would be willing to bet that he is just not financially stable. If he offers to go 'Dutch' then I recommend you ditch this guy ASAP because he is obviously not willing to invest the money to get to know you.

I think many people embellish their incomes as well on the dating profiles. They simply think they will have a better shot for a date if they say they make more money than they do. Then again to be fair, there are the people that are totally up front about how much money they make and they have no reason to hide anything.

# People Are Lonely

There are people out there that will embellish their income on their profiles simply because they are lonely and this goes for both Men and Women. They are just very lonely or needy and only want someone in their lives and will do anything to have it. For women that make a lot of money they should watch out for the guy that will seek her out only for her money because they do not have a job or are so stretched that they are looking to find someone to pay for all of their needs this could be their rent, cell phone, cars, boats, back child support, court fines or other things. This is almost always something a guy will not disclose until he thinks he has you right where he wants you. After he thinks he has you, these things will come up. Unfortunately, you will need to date this person awhile before you figure this out. If this is OK with you then more power to you but you take a risk that if they find someone with more money, they will simply leave you to go to greener pastures. This is why I believe that if you are a woman, you should find someone that is on the same level as you are financially. Or, if they have some struggles and everyone goes through struggles make sure they are responsible enough to take care of themselves and their obligations. A big red flag would be if the guy has child support obligations that they do not meet. (Dead Beat Dad). If they are not willing or able to fulfill financially supporting their children then they have no business spending money on anything else and they are just not responsible people.

## For the Men

Women will lie about their income or financial obligations the same way a man will. For a man, you will need to decide if you are willing to take on a woman who has a lot of financial obligations. For example, they may have a lot of Credit Card debt. This is something to pay attention to because maybe they are irresponsible with their money and like to shop a lot. As a woman, I totally understand wanting to shop and I have done my share but I can pay for what I buy. Luckily I learned to be responsible with my money and that is not always easy to do but I was a single mother for many years and I did not want anyone to know how much I struggled with money. As my kids got older I got a better paying job and was more financially secure.

Custody obligations. This is something to REALLY pay attention to. If a woman does not have at least 50% of custody of her children then there could be a problem. As a woman I believe in supporting your kids and if you meet a woman who has very little, supervised or no custody of their children then there is a dam good reason why and I guarantee you that is not a good thing. She could be an addict, have a criminal record or worse child neglect issues. This is not a good thing and is something you should ask about before you go out with this person. If I were a man and I wanted to date a woman with children, I would want to know if they have any kind of custody with their children and if they don't, I would choose not to go out with this person. Remember, this is not something that they will disclose or may lie about so you may have to date this person in order to find out.

# *10*

# *STD's*

## Sexually Transmitted Diseases

This is not something that is easy to talk about for anyone with a STD. Before you become intimate with anyone you meet online and I highly suggest you be in a monogamous relationship before you do, you will need to discuss any STD's you may have. This is the responsible thing to do and many people will not disclose their STD history for fear of being rejected. This is a big reason why the STD's keep getting spread among people because people do not want to tell anyone they have a STD. Lying about having a STD is a very dangerous thing. It is irresponsible and shows lack of compassion or regard to their partner. This is why when you are dating online you will need to be very careful of what you do and who you do it with. Just because someone looks clean and is a good person doesn't mean that they do not have a STD. Life happens and sometimes things just don't go the way we planned. I don't know anyone that would intentionally ask for a STD do you?

According to the Centers for Disease Control and Prevention (CDC), approximately 19 million new sexually transmitted infections occur each year, almost half of them among young people aged 15 to 24. This doesn't mean that if you are over 24, you can have sex without protection!

I want to bring this up because it is important. It is a fact that heterosexual men sometimes cheat with gay males. Does that make them bisexual? I'm not sure (and it really doesn't matter) the fact is that for some reason they think this is OK and this is also something that they will not disclose or flat out lie about and who knows if they use protection. I wouldn't want to be on the receiving end of a guy like that. You cannot be too careful!

Remember, anyone you meet on an Online Dating site is a total stranger. Don't get your emotions all worked up over someone you don't know. Some people (mostly women) are just natural 'givers'. They will give themselves to any guy just because they think they can get a guy to commit. I have a news flash but women that give sex on the first date or soon after are more likely to get 'dumped' by the guy because he is out for one thing and once he gets it, he loses interest fast. And yes, the guys will tell you practically anything (lies) to get you to do what they want. Ladies, don't give yourself away until the guy earns it! You will be highly disappointed and could end up with an STD, pregnant or even physically harmed. This is why you need to date someone for a while to get to know them to protect yourself as much as you possibly can.

This can become a legal issue as well. Let's talk about a woman who was awarded $900,000 in Oregon from a man that gave her a STD.  She met this man on E-Harmony.com. She asked him to wear a condom and he agreed but he never used one and after their encounter he disclosed he had a STD. By this time it was too late for her so she sued him and won in 2012. He also got charged for 'battery' because he intentionally harmed her.

For many people as they get older, (over 40) they do not think much about STD's. Most likely they have been married and divorced for many years therefore they are not looking to have children. They think that it is something that happens when you are young but they are sadly mistaken. If you're planning to start a relationship with someone, go together and get tested for STDs. Anyone who has more than one sexual partner should be tested at least once a year for STDs. If you are at all concerned that you may have acquired an STD, it makes sense to see your doctor.

# Key facts

- ✓ More than 1 million people acquire a sexually transmitted disease (STD) every day.
- ✓ Each year, an estimated 500 million people become ill with one of 4 STDs: chlamydia, gonorrhea, syphilis and trichomoniasis.
- ✓ More than 530 million people have the virus that causes genital herpes (HSV2). There is no cure.
- ✓ More than 290 million women have a human papillomavirus (HPV) infection.
- ✓ The majority of STDs are present without symptoms.
- ✓ Some STDs can increase the risk of HIV acquisition three-fold or more.
- ✓ STDs can have serious consequences beyond the immediate impact of the infection itself, through mother-to-child transmission of infections and chronic diseases.

## My Advice

It is a crime if you know you have an STD and pass it on to someone else without informing them first. If you have a STD, please be responsible and notify the other person before getting intimate. You may be surprised that hundreds of thousands of Online Daters have a STD and will never disclose this information to you. Always practice safe sex no matter how old or young you are!  Condoms and other protection can greatly reduce the risk of most sexually transmitted diseases, but even these are not 100 percent effective.